New Zealand Fun Facts Picture Book for Kids

An Educational City Travel Photography Photobook About History, Places with Everything You Need to Know About the Country for Children

Geography

New Zealand is an island country in the south-western Pacific Ocean. It consists of two main islands-The North and the South Island and approximately 700 other islands. The South Island houses Mount Cook, the highest mountain peak in the country.

New Zealand has over 50 Volcanoes, and some are still active presently. The closest country to New Zealand is Australia, and Wellington is its capital city.

New Zealand fun facts

The town with the longest name, Taumatawhakatangihangakoauauotamateaturi pukakapikimaungahoronukupokaiwhenuakitan atahu is located in New Zealand.

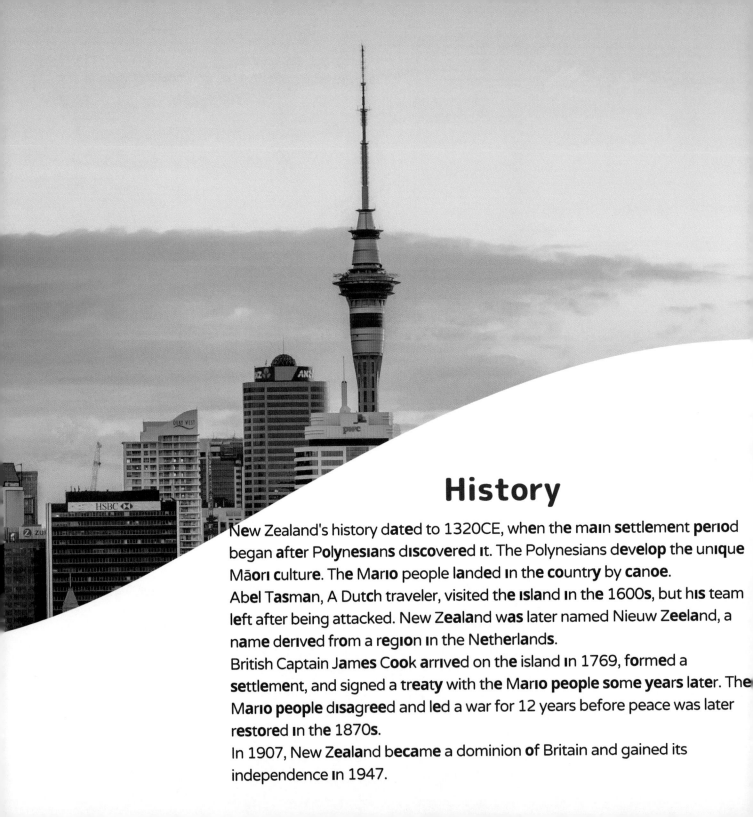

History

New Zealand's history dated to 1320CE, when the main settlement period began after Polynesians discovered it. The Polynesians develop the unique Māori culture. The Mario people landed in the country by canoe.

Abel Tasman, A Dutch traveler, visited the island in the 1600s, but his team left after being attacked. New Zealand was later named Nieuw Zeeland, a name derived from a region in the Netherlands.

British Captain James Cook arrived on the island in 1769, formed a settlement, and signed a treaty with the Mario people some years later. The Mario people disagreed and led a war for 12 years before peace was later restored in the 1870s.

In 1907, New Zealand became a dominion of Britain and gained its independence in 1947.

NEW ZEALAND FUN FACTS

New Zealand was the last country to be inhabited by humans.

Climate

New Zealand's Climate and Weather vary and can be unpredictable due to its diverse landscape. You can experience four seasons in 24 hours, as locals often say. But Generally, New Zealand has moderate weather and temperature. The winters are mild, and summers are relatively cool. January and February are the warmest months of the year and the coldest month is July.

People

The people of New Zealand are mainly Europeans. Māori, Asian, Pacific people, and Africans are other ethnicities in the country. Geographically, the majority of the population lives on the North Island.

New Zealand has three official languages: English, New Zealand Sign Language, and The Māori Language(Te Reo Māori). New Zealanders speak very fast and have a strong accent with slang words.

Christianity is the most popular religion in New Zealand. Hinduism, Islam, and Buddhism are also religions that can be found there. New Zealanders are friendly and humble people. They also show hospitality to strangers or foreigners.

NEW ZEALAND FUN FACTS

New Zealand was the first country to give women the right to vote.

Culture

Māori is the indigenous people of New Zealand, so the Māori culture is the central part of the country's culture. It affects the language, arts, and accents. The Māori people show love for sport, arts, and outdoor activities.

Generally, New Zealand is known for rugby, sheep, kiwi fruit, wine, Manuka honey, stargazing, and adventure sports.

Economy

A large part of the New Zealand economy depends on Tourism, with over two million visitors annually. The service sector and the agriculture sectors are growing as well. The major exports are kiwi fruit, wine, lamb, and butter. The New Zealand dollar(NZD) is the country's currency.

NEW ZEALAND FUN FACTS

New Zealand is home to the clearest water in the World.

Public Holidays

Eleven public holidays in New Zealand are recognized nationwide. If any public holiday falls on Sunday, Monday is usually considered a holiday.

New Year's Day-Jan 1st
Day after New Year's Day-Jan 1-4
Waitangi Day- Feb 7
Easter Holidays (Good Friday and Easter Monday)
Anzac Day- Apr 25
Queen's Birthday- Jun 6
Matariki- Jun 24
Labor Day-Oct 24
Christmas Holidays (Christmas and Boxing Day).

Each region also celebrates its anniversary day.

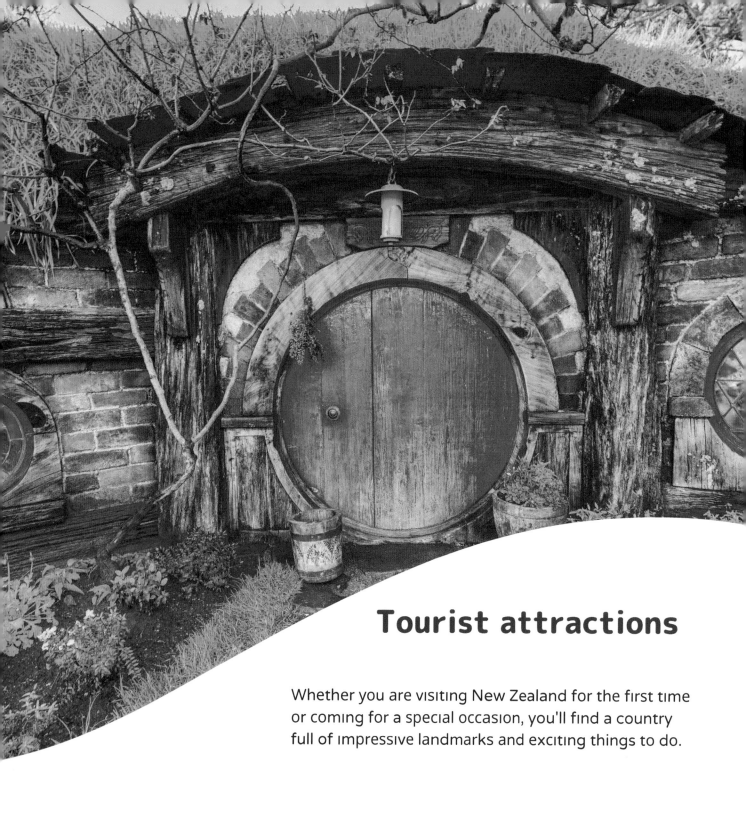

Tourist attractions

Whether you are visiting New Zealand for the first time or coming for a special occasion, you'll find a country full of impressive landmarks and exciting things to do.

Fiordland National Park

Located on the South Island, it consists of some beautiful places in New Zealand, such as the Fjords of Milford. A visit here means exploring virgin rain forests, lakes, islands, and mountains.

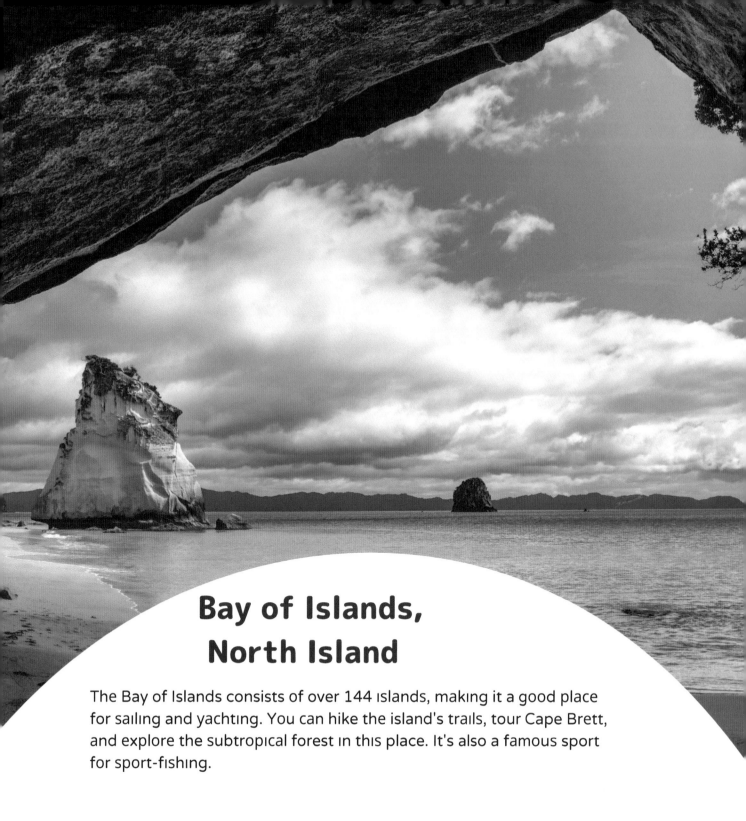

Bay of Islands, North Island

The Bay of Islands consists of over 144 islands, making it a good place for sailing and yachting. You can hike the island's trails, tour Cape Brett, and explore the subtropical forest in this place. It's also a famous sport for sport-fishing.

Tongariro
National Park

One of the World's oldest national parks, it's a land of natural wonders and stunning beauty. Towering volcanoes, arid players, herb fields, and turquoise lakes are some things you will see there.

Rotorua

Rotorua is located in the Pacific Ring of Fire, so it's home to geothermal wonders.
Some of the wonders you will see there include Boiling mud pools, steaming geysers,
volcanic craters, and hissing thermal springs.

Coromandel Peninsula

The Coromandel Peninsula is located in Northern New Zealand. This tourist attraction is an excellent place to get away from the city's noise and crowding and enjoy a peaceful environment. It has beaches, and you will experience hiking, skydiving, and kayaking.

Queenstown

Queenstown is a popular tourist place in New Zealand. It has a lot of amazing activities to enjoy, including Jet boating, Bungee jumping, Rock climbing, downhill skiing, white-water rafting, and many more fun activities.

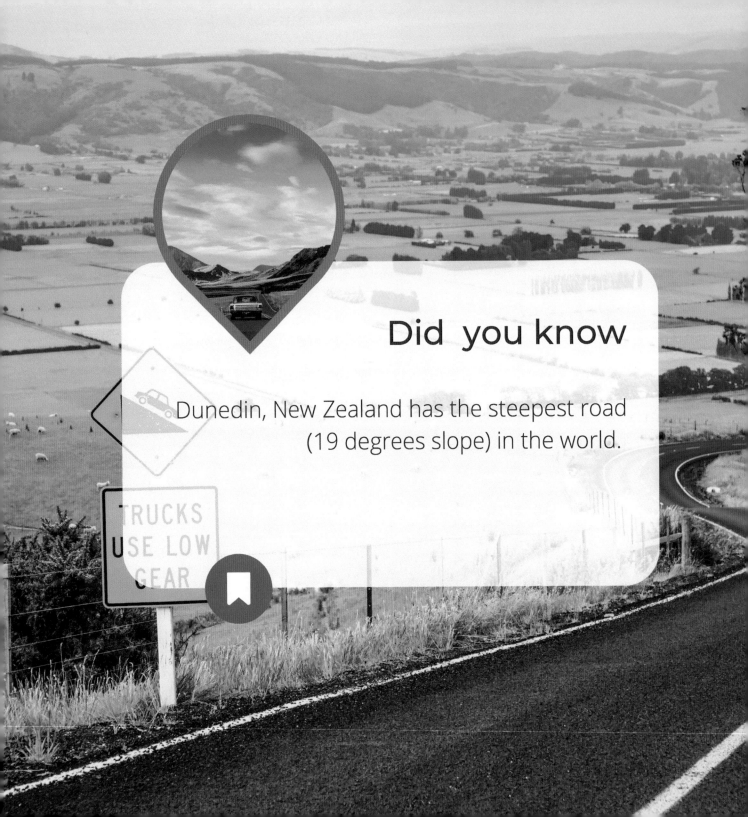

Did you know

Dunedin, New Zealand has the steepest road (19 degrees slope) in the world.

Festivals

The best way to experience New Zealand is through its unique festivals. Festivals in New Zealand mostly celebrate culture, art, or religion.

Popular annual events and festivals

Pasifika Cultural Festival: every first week of March annually, The Pasifika focuses on Pacific Island communities in the country. Visitors experience various cultures from Fiji, Hawaii, Tahiti, and more through art, music, dance, and food events.

Auckland Lantern Festival: Held every February between 13 and 16, The Auckland Lantern festival's celebration is for the Chinese New Year, so visitors enjoy different cultures. Albert Park is lit up with lanterns, and there are fireworks shows .

Traditional Māori Kai Festivals: The Māori Kai festivals are a series of festivals that occur every year across the nation that involves the best Māori food like pork, mussels, oysters, and kababs.

Womad Festival: Womad Festival is an award-winning festival in New Zealand that brings artists from different parts of the world for top performances and collaboration with various cultures.

Rhythm and Vines: artists and stars perform their collection of music in this annual celebration. The festival is a fun way to enjoy the New Year.

Museums

New Zealand has some of the most important museums in the world, and it would be wrong not to visit at least one.

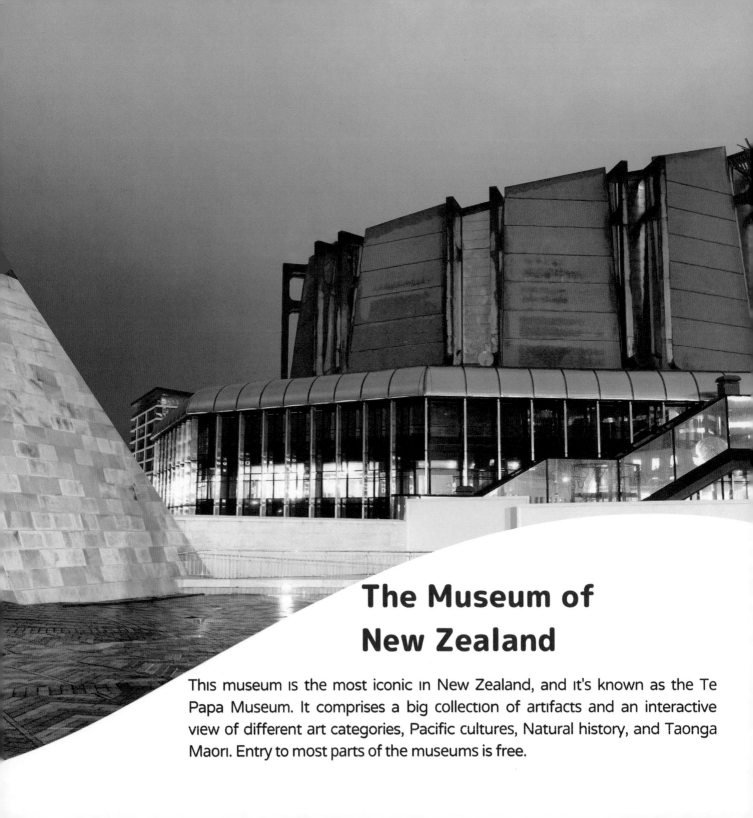

The Museum of New Zealand

This museum is the most iconic in New Zealand, and it's known as the Te Papa Museum. It comprises a big collection of artifacts and an interactive view of different art categories, Pacific cultures, Natural history, and Taonga Maori. Entry to most parts of the museums is free.

Otago Museum

The Otago Museum will expose you to the stories of culture, science, and nature of the Otago region and international discoveries. The main exhibition and galleries at the museum are free except for Tubura Science Center in it.

Omaka Aviation Heritage Center

Omaka Aviation Heritage center presents a great collection of warplanes in an exciting way. In the museum, you will see the planes and memorabilia of both World War collections of Sir Peter Jackson in realistic static displays.

Auckland War Memorial Museum

The Auckland War Memorial Museum is a museum with great architectural design. It is home to an impressive collection of Maori art while showcasing the story of Auckland's people and culture. The museum's top floor is dedicated to the Military of New Zealand.

Food and Dining

New Zealand foods are a mix of Asia, Europe, and Polynesia food, so they are mouth-watering. New Zealand-style dishes include lamb, salmon, pork, crayfish, white sir, kiwi fruit, oysters, and Shellfish. Barbeques are also a big part of the Kiwi culture.

New Zealanders like to eat their food in a gentle and relaxed manner like the Kiwi culture.

Accommodation

New Zealand accommodation options are plentiful. You'll find luxurious lodge accommodation in the country's main centers where you can view the native and beautiful scenery.

Accommodation options in New Zealand include luxury lodges, glamping accommodation, hotels, motels, back-to-nature camping, Holiday parks, and campgrounds.

Transportation

The options for transportation are numerous. From trains and trams to buses and taxis, you are faced with quality options to travel around the country. Here are transportation options in New Zealand.

Trains

In New Zealand, Train transportation is not common, but three major train lines operate: Auckland-Wellington, Christchurch-West Coast, and Picton-Christchurch.

Bus

Buses are the most common form of public transportation in New Zealand. They are cheap and available across cities and towns.

Taxis

Taxi and Uber transportation is available if you don't like public transport or prefer privacy. You can download the Uber app from your phone App store.

Ferry

Ferries are a common transportation mode between the North and South Islands. You can find a ferry at other places, including Mainland, New Zealand offshore island, and Stewart Island.

Water Taxi

Water Taxis offer easy transportation to places ferries can not reach. Such places include small ports and hiking and biking spots. Water Taxi services are usually scheduled.

Planes

The plane is popular for longer trips in New Zealand, especially for business or personal travel.

Shopping

Shopping in New Zealand is a great experience. Depending on your budget, there is a long list of gifts and items to buy. New Zealand cities and towns have shopping outlets, malls, and arcades where you can get your desired stuff. Some popular things to buy in New Zealand include ornaments and jewelry, beautiful merino, handcrafted glass, and fashion accessories.

NEW ZEALAND FUN FACTS

There are more sheep than people in New Zealand.

When to Visit New Zealand?

The best time to visit New Zealand is in Autumn when there are fewer crowds and the days are sunny. The weather is usually warm between March-May, and the accommodation rates are low. If you want to enjoy snow sports, Winter is the best time to visit. However, Summer visitation is the most popular in New Zealand.

Auckland city, New Zealand

Printed in Great Britain
by Amazon

21652106R10025